The First Five Minutes With a Car Buyer

How to Turn a Greeting into a Real Sales Conversation

Bruce Huddleston

Bedrock Heritage Publishing

The First Five Minutes With a Car Buyer

How to Transition from Greeting to Conversation and Move Toward the Sale

Copyright © 2026 by Bedrock Heritage Publishing

All rights reserved.

No part of this publication may be reproduced, distributed, or transmitted in any form or by any means, including photocopying, recording, or other electronic or mechanical methods, without the prior written permission of the publisher, except for brief quotations in reviews or critical articles.

Author: Bruce Huddleston

Series: Car Sales Survival Guide Series — Book 10 of 10

Publisher: Bedrock Heritage Publishing, A Division of Life Guidance Consulting LLC, Tyler, Texas

ISBN: 978-1-972179-18-5 (Paperback)

ISBN: 978-1-972179-71-0 (EPUB)

Manufactured in the United States of America

DISCLAIMER

This book is based on the author's personal and professional experiences, observations, and opinions, accumulated over a 35-year career in the automotive industry. It is intended for educational and informational purposes only.

The stories and anecdotes contained in this book are drawn from real-world situations encountered throughout the author's career. However, names, identifying details, specific circumstances, employer names, dealership names, and individual characteristics have been changed, omitted, combined, or fictionalized to protect the privacy of the individuals involved. Any resemblance to specific living persons, current or former employers, or existing businesses is coincidental and unintentional.

No individual, dealership, organization, or employer referenced or implied in the stories within this book has reviewed, approved, or endorsed the content herein. The recollections and characterizations presented are solely the author's own perspective and memory of events and do not constitute a factual record, legal testimony, or statement of fact regarding any identifiable person or entity.

The sales strategies, techniques, and professional advice presented in this book reflect the author's personal approach and experience. Individual results will vary based on experience, effort, market conditions, dealership policies, and other factors beyond the author's control. Nothing in this book constitutes a guarantee of income, employment, or professional outcome.

To every salesperson who ever nailed the hello and then froze, with no idea what came next.

I was you. I stalled. I pitched too early. I interrogated good people right off the lot and then told myself they were just looking.

This book is the thing I wish somebody had handed me back then. It's for you.

A Free Bonus For Readers

Your Complete Digital Script Library

Get the Car Sales Survival Quick-Reference Card — a free companion to this book that puts the key rules and techniques on one page you can keep at your desk.

Visit:

www.carsalessurvivalseries.com/scripts

Enter your email to claim your free reader bonus.
Print it. Keep it. Use it.

Contents

Introduction

The First Five Minutes Decide Where the Deal Goes

The greeting is over. You walked up the right way, you didn't crowd them, you didn't sprint across the lot sweating through your shirt, and the customer is standing there in front of you, willing to talk. So now what?

That question — that "now what" — is the whole book.

Here's what nobody told me when I started. I spent years thinking the sale was won at the close. Thinking it all came down to the numbers, the pencil, the back-and-forth in the box. I was wrong. By the time you get to the numbers, the deal is mostly already decided. It got decided way back at the beginning, in the four or five minutes right after hello, when the customer was sizing me up and figuring out whether I was somebody worth talking to or just one more guy trying to put them in a car today.

The greeting gets you in the door. That's all it does. It buys you a few minutes of the customer's attention and a little bit of their patience. What you do with those minutes is everything.

Most salespeople have no idea what to do with them. I sure didn't. I'd nail the hello and then freeze. Or worse — I'd fill the silence with a pitch nobody asked for, or start firing questions like I was running a background check. Budget? Trade? Financing? Buying today? I ran customers off by the dozen and told myself they were just looking.

They weren't just looking. They were just leaving. There's a difference, and I caused it.

This book is about the bridge. The greeting is on one side. A real sales conversation â€” a customer talking, opening up, telling you what they actually came in for â€” is the other side. The first five minutes are the bridge between them, and most salespeople fall straight off it.

We're going to cross it on purpose. I'm going to show you the moves, one at a time. The hand-off is when you turn a greeting into an actual conversation. The opening question that gets people talking instead of shutting them down. The listening â€” and I mean real listening, because that's the spine of this whole thing. How to find the real reason they came, which is rarely the reason they say first. How to build trust that's worth a damn, not canned small talk. How to read the customer and match their pace instead of running your script over them. And how to keep things moving, gently, no pressure, toward the next step.

We're going to stop at the threshold. This isn't a closing book. We end where the real sales process begins â€” the customer in the car, the deal in motion. The first five minutes don't close anybody. They decide whether there will be a deal to close at all.

This is the last book in the series. Books 1 through 8 got you to the customer and gave you the nerve to approach. Book 9 cleaned up the greeting. This one takes a good greeting and turns it into a moving, productive conversation that points straight at the sale. It's where it all comes together.

So the greeting went well. Good. Now, let's turn the next five minutes into a deal in motion.

"The Rule: The greeting gets you in the door. The next five minutes decide whether there's a deal behind it."

Chapter 1

The Hand-Off: Turning a Greeting Into a Conversation

Here's the most common place a deal dies, and it dies quiet. The salesperson greets the customer just fine — smiles, says hello, gets it right — and then nothing. The handshake ends, and both people are just standing there. Awkward silence. The salesperson panics and does one of two things. They go quiet and let the customer drift off, or they lurch into a pitch. Both kill it.

That gap, right after hello, is where the hand-off happens. The hand-off is the move that turns a greeting into a conversation. It's the most important five seconds of the first five minutes, and almost nobody practices it.

I didn't, for years. I treated the greeting like the finish line. Got the hello right, felt good about it, and then stood there like a fence post waiting for the customer to do the work. They never did. Why would they? They didn't come in to carry the conversation. That's my job.

What the Hand-Off Actually Is

The hand-off is simple. After you say hello, you hand the customer something easy to respond to — a low-pressure opening that invites them to talk without demanding anything. You're not asking for their budget. You're not asking if they're buying today. You're giving them an easy on-ramp into a conversation and then getting out of the way.

The keyword is easy. The customer just walked up with their guard partway up. They're expecting pressure — everybody expects pressure at a car lot. The hand-off is your chance to show them this is going to be different. You do that by making the first thing out of your mouth after hello sound like something a normal person would say, not something off a script.

Why It Goes Wrong

Most failed hand-offs come from one of two fears. The first is the fear of silence, which makes salespeople talk too much, too fast, about the wrong things. The second is the fear of the customer, which makes them go stiff and formal and start interrogating.

Picture it from the customer's side. They walked in cautious. They're ready to be sold. Then the salesperson either won't stop talking or starts demanding information before they've earned a single answer. What does the customer do? They reach for the oldest shield there is. "We're just looking." And now you've lost them — not because the greeting was bad, but because the hand-off never happened.

FROM THE FLOOR

I walked into a well-known furniture store one afternoon looking for a recliner. Had a specific one in mind. Knew what I wanted to spend. Ready to buy. Three salespeople were sitting on a showroom couch. I could hear them — in earshot, not trying to be quiet — debating whose turn it was to help me. Like I was an interruption to whatever they had going on.

The one who drew the short straw walked over. No greeting. No name. No smile. Just: "What are you here to buy today?"

I said: "Nothing. I'm just looking. I'll let you know if I need help."

And I meant it. They'd lost me in the first five seconds. I didn't buy a thing there. Went somewhere else and bought the same recliner the same afternoon.

The irony is, I walked in ready to spend money. All they had to do was make me feel like a person instead of a chore. Instead, they spent more energy arguing over whose turn it was than they spent on the customer standing in front of them. That's not a sales problem. That's a culture problem. And it starts—and ends—with how a team treats the greeting.

Read that one again, because I lived it from the customer's side, and it taught me everything. I walked in ready to spend money. All they had to do was hand me a conversation. Instead, they handed me a chore — "What are you here to buy today?" — and I was gone in five seconds. That's a failed hand-off. No greeting worth the name, no on-ramp, just a demand. It happens on car lots every single day.

How to Do It Right

After hello, lead with something that lowers the temperature. Acknowledge them as a person before you ask anything of them. "Glad you came in — what's got you out looking today?" is a hand-off. "Are you buying today?" is an ambush. One opens a door. The other slams it.

Then — and this is the part nobody does — you stop talking. You hand it off, and you let them take it. The silence you were so scared of? Let it sit for a second. Give them room to answer. The hand-off isn't you performing. It's you opening a door and stepping back so they can walk through it.

Get the hand-off right, and you're not standing in awkward silence anymore. You're in a conversation. Everything else in this book builds on that.

"The Rule: A greeting isn't a conversation. The hand-off is the move that turns one into the other."

CHAPTER 2

THE OPENING QUESTION: HOW TO GET THEM TALKING

THE HAND-OFF NEEDS SOMETHING to hand off. That something is a question. Not just any question — the opening question. Get it right, and the customer starts talking. Get it wrong, and they give you one word and look at their phone.

I learned the hard way that the question you ask first sets the whole tone. For a long time, my go-to was "Can I help you find something?" You know what that gets you? "No thanks, just looking." Every time. I trained customers to brush me off with my own bad question.

Open Questions vs. Closing Questions

There are two kinds of questions, and you need to know the difference cold.

A closing question can be answered with one word. "Can I help you?" — No. "Looking for a truck?" — No. "Buying today?" — No. Every closing question hands the customer an exit, and a nervous customer takes it.

An open question can't be answered in one word. It needs a sentence. "What's got you out looking today?" "What are you hoping to find?" "Tell me what's going on with your current vehicle." These don't have a one-word escape hatch. They invite a story. And the second the customer starts telling you a story, you're in a real conversation.

My Favorite Opening Question

If I could only ask one question for the rest of my life, it'd be some version of this: "What's got you out today?"

It's casual. It's warm. It assumes nothing. It doesn't ask if they're buying, doesn't ask their budget, doesn't box them in. It just opens the floor. And the answer — whatever it is — gives you somewhere to go.

What to Do With the Answer

Here's the part people miss. The opening question is worthless if you don't do anything with the answer. Most salespeople ask a decent question and then completely ignore the response because they're already thinking about their next line.

Don't do that. The answer to your opening question is the most valuable thing you're going to get in the first five minutes. It's the thread. You pull on it. They say, "My truck finally died on me" — you don't jump to "great, let me show you our trucks." You say, "Ah, what happened?" and you let them tell you. Every follow-up should come from what they just said, not from your script.

Picture it from their side. They expected a sales pitch. Instead, somebody asked them an easy question and then actually listened to the answer and asked more. That's not what they braced for. That's a relief. And a relieved customer talks.

One question, asked right, followed up honestly, and you've got momentum. That's all the opening question has to do.

"The Rule: Ask the question that opens a door, not the one that slams it. 'What's got you out today' beats 'What are you here to buy' every time."

CHAPTER 3

LISTEN FIRST: THE FIRST FIVE MINUTES BELONG TO THE CUSTOMER

THIS IS THE MOST important chapter in the book. If you take one thing from all of this, take this: the first five minutes belong to the customer, not to you. Your job in those minutes is to shut up and listen.

I know that's not what you were taught. I wasn't taught that either. I was taught to control the conversation, to lead, to always be talking, to never let a silence sit. So I talked. I talked over customers, I talked past them, I talked myself right out of deals. It took me years to figure out that the best salesperson on the lot was usually the quietest one in the first five minutes.

Why Listening Outsells Talking

When you talk, you learn nothing. You already know everything you're saying. The only way to find out what the customer actually needs — the thing that's going to make this deal happen — is to let them tell you. And they will tell you, if you give them room. People want to be heard. A customer who feels heard will hand you the whole deal on a plate.

The salesperson who listens first outsells the one who talks first. Every time. Not because listening is polite — though it is — but because listening is how you find out what you're actually selling.

What Real Listening Looks Like

Real listening isn't waiting for your turn to talk. Most "listening" on a car lot is just a salesperson holding their breath until the customer stops so they can launch their pitch. The customer can feel that. They know when you're loading up instead of listening.

Real listening looks like this. You ask your opening question. They answer. You don't respond with a pitch — you respond with a follow-up that proves you heard them. "You said the back seat's too tight for the car seats — how many are we fitting back there?" That tells the customer you caught the detail that mattered to them. Now they trust you a little more. Now they tell you more.

It also looks like silence. When the customer finishes a thought, don't rush to fill the air. Wait. Half the time, they'll keep going, and the second thing they say is more honest than the first.

Listening Earns the Right to Talk

Here's the trade. You listen first, and that earns you the right to talk later. Once a customer has told you what they need — and felt you actually hear it — they'll listen to you when it's your turn, because you've shown them you're not just running a script over the top of them.

Flip it to the customer's side one more time. They walked in expecting to be talked at. Instead, somebody asked a real question and then got quiet and actually listened to the answer. Do you know how rare that is? It's so rare that it builds more trust in two minutes than an hour of charm ever could.

Talk less. Listen more. The first five minutes belong to them.

"The Rule: The first five minutes belong to the customer. The salesperson who listens first outsells the one who talks first."

Chapter 4

FINDING THE REAL REASON THEY CAME

NOBODY WALKS ONTO A car lot for no reason. Something pushed them out the door today instead of last month or next month. That something — the real reason they came — is the whole deal. Find it, and everything gets easier. Miss it, and you're selling blind.

Here's the catch. The reason they give you first is almost never the real one. "Just looking at trucks." Okay. But why today? What happened? There's always a why under the why, and your job in the first five minutes is to find it.

The Surface Answer vs. the Real Trigger

The surface answer is what they say. "I'm looking at SUVs." The real trigger is what's underneath it. The new baby. The transmission that just went out and isn't worth fixing. The promotion that finally made room in the budget. The teenager who just got a license. The reason underneath is emotional, it's specific, and it's the thing that's actually going to move them to buy.

A customer who says, "I'm looking at something with more room" might be telling you about a third kid on the way. That's not a vehicle preference. That's a life event. And if you understand the life event, you understand the customer — what they need, what they're worried about, what's going to make them feel good about saying yes.

How to Get Under the Surface

You don't get there by interrogating. You get there by listening and asking gentle follow-ups about what they've already told you. They say, "We need more space." You say, "Yeah? What's changed?" That's it. That little open door — "what's changed" — lets them tell you the real story if they want to. Usually, they want to. People like talking about their lives more than they like talking about cars.

And when they tell you, you acknowledge it before you do anything else. That's the move. Not "great, let me show you the three-row models." First: "Congratulations — that's a great reason to be car shopping." You meet them where they are. Then you help.

FROM THE FLOOR

The summer heat in Texas is no joke. I was managing a used car lot — no air conditioning on the lot, obviously — and it was one of those July afternoons where the asphalt is soft, and the air feels like a wet towel. A couple pulled in. I watched my newest salesperson sprint out to meet them — which was already the wrong move — and by the time he got to them, he was visibly sweating through his shirt. The customers looked at him, looked at each other, and said they were just looking. He came back inside looking defeated.

I went out. Introduced myself. Said: "Sorry about the heat — let me know if you want to step inside and cool off while we talk." That's all it took. They came inside. We sold them a car in ninety minutes. The first salesperson did everything wrong before he said a word. I did one thing right: I acknowledged where they were before I asked anything of them.

Look at what actually happened there. My salesperson treated it like a transaction and got "just looking." I treated the customer like a person standing in the heat — I acknowledged where they actually were before I asked them for anything — and that one move opened the whole conversation. Acknowledging the customer's real situation is how you get under the surface. It's the same with a customer who just totaled their car, or just had a baby, or just got their hours cut, and needs something cheaper to run. Meet the situation first. The selling comes after.

Why the Real Reason Is the Whole Deal

When you know the real reason, you stop guessing. You're not throwing vehicles at the wall hoping one sticks. You're solving the actual problem that brought them in. And the customer feels it — they feel like you get it, like you're on their side, like this is the rare salesperson who's trying to help instead of just trying to sell.

Nobody buys a car. They buy what the car fixes. Find what they're trying to fix, and you've found the deal.

"The Rule: Nobody buys a car. They buy what the car fixes. Find the real reason they came, and you've found the deal."

CHAPTER 5

BUILDING REAL TRUST, NOT SMALL TALK

SOMEWHERE ALONG THE LINE, somebody taught salespeople that building rapport means small talk. Ask where they're from. Compliment the jacket. Talk about the weather. Find some common ground and chit-chat until they like you. I did all of that for years. It's mostly a waste of everybody's time, and worse, the customer can smell it.

Real trust isn't built with small talk. It's built by being a real person and proving you actually heard them. That's a different thing entirely, and it's the thing that makes the rest of the deal possible.

Why Small Talk Falls Flat

The problem with canned rapport is that it's obvious. When you ask "so where are y'all from?" with that practiced salesman warmth, the customer knows exactly what you're doing. You're running the rapport step. It's on a checklist somewhere, and they can feel it. It doesn't make them trust you. It makes them brace harder because now they know you've got a routine and they're standing in the middle of it.

Customers have a finely tuned radar for fake. They've been sold to their whole lives. The second you sound like a technique instead of a person, the guard goes right back up.

Be a Person First

The fix is simpler than the problem. Just be a person. Drop the routine and react like a human being to whatever the customer actually says. If they mention they just got off work, you don't run the "where do you work" script to fish for income — you say "long day?" because that's what a person says. If their kid is bouncing off the walls, you smile at the kid instead of pretending the kid isn't there.

Being a person first means your interest is real, not performed. You're not collecting rapport points. You're talking to somebody. That comes across, and it's worth ten times the canned version.

Trust Buys Honest Answers

Here's why this matters for the deal, not just for being a decent human. Trust in the first five minutes buys you honest answers later. A customer who trusts you tells you the truth about their budget, their trade, their credit situation, what they're really worried about. A customer who doesn't trust you lies to you — not because they're bad people, but because they're protecting themselves from somebody they don't trust.

Every honest answer you get later was bought by the trust you built early. And you don't build that trust by talking about the weather. You build it by listening, by reacting like a real person, and by showing them — in those first few minutes — that you're on their side.

It Doesn't Take Long

People think trust takes a long time. In the first five minutes, you don't have a long time, and you don't need it. Trust early on isn't about depth — it's about signal. A handful of small, genuine moments where the customer thinks "okay, this one's actually listening" is enough to change the whole tone.

You're not trying to become their friend in five minutes. You're trying to prove you're worth being honest with. That's a much lower bar, and you clear it by being real.

"The Rule: Trust isn't built with small talk. It's built by being a real person and proving you actually heard them."

CHAPTER 6

READING THE CUSTOMER AND MATCHING THEIR PACE

READING THE **C**USTOMER AND Matching Their Pace

Not every customer wants the same thing from you. Some walk onto the lot ready to move — they know what they want, they want it handled, and the worst thing you can do is slow them down with chitchat. Others need room. They want to look, to think, to circle the lot twice before they say a word. Run the same approach on both, and you'll lose one of them every time.

The skill is reading which one you've got, fast, and matching their pace instead of running your own over the top of them.

Read the Signals

You can usually tell within the first minute. The customer who walks straight to a specific vehicle and starts asking pointed questions is telling you they're ready to move — give them answers, not a relationship. The customer who wanders, who keeps their answers short, who won't quite make eye contact yet, is telling you they need space — give them room and let them warm up.

Watch the body language. Watch the pace they walk. Listen to how much they give you when you ask a question. A one-word answer isn't rudeness —

it's information. It's telling you to back off the gas a little. A flood of detail is information too — it's telling you they're comfortable and you can keep going.

Match, Don't Override

Once you've read the pace, match it. If they're fast and direct, be fast and direct back. Don't make a customer who's ready to buy sit through your relationship-building routine — you'll frustrate them right out the door. If they're slow and cautious, slow down. Don't push a hesitant customer to move faster than they're ready to. Pressure on a cautious customer doesn't speed them up. It makes them leave.

I had to learn this the hard way, because early on, I had exactly one speed. I ran the same approach on everybody, and I couldn't figure out why it worked great on some people and bombed on others. It wasn't them. It was me, refusing to read the room.

When There's More Than One of Them

Often you've got more than one person — a couple, a family. Now you've got more than one pace to read, and more than one person to keep in the conversation. Pay attention to who's quiet. The person who isn't talking is frequently the one who'll decide whether this happens, and if they feel ignored, they'll shut the whole thing down later, quietly, in the car on the way home.

So include everybody. Ask each of them what they think. Notice who looks at whom before answering — that tells you where the real weight sits. You're not trying to figure out who to sell and who to ignore. You're trying to make sure nobody standing there feels run over. A customer who feels heard says yes. A customer who feels ignored finds a reason to say no.

Stay Flexible

Don't lock in your read too early. The quiet one might warm all the way up once they trust you. The fast one might slow down when it gets real. Keep reading the whole time and keep adjusting. Matching the customer's pace isn't a one-time decision at the start — it's something you do the entire first five minutes, and well beyond.

"The Rule: Match the customer's pace, not your script. The fast ones want answers; the slow ones want room. Give them theirs, not yours."

CHAPTER 7

"I'm Just Looking": Keeping the Door Open

SALESPEOPLE, IT LANDS LIKE a door slamming. It feels like rejection — like the customer has already decided they don't want your help. So they either give up and walk away, or they panic and push. Both are wrong.

"I'm just looking" is not a verdict. It's information. And once you understand what it's actually telling you, it stops being scary.

What They're Really Saying

Most of the time, "I'm just looking" means one thing: I don't trust you yet, and I'm protecting myself from pressure. That's it. It's a shield. The customer walked in expecting to get pounced on, and "just looking" is the thing they say to keep some space between themselves and the hard sell they're braced for.

It is almost never a real statement about their intentions. Plenty of people who say "just looking" buy a car that same afternoon. They said it out of habit, out of self-protection, before they'd decided one thing about you. So don't take it as the final word. Take it as the opening line.

Keep the Door Open

The right response is calm, short, and pressure-free. "Perfect — take all the time you want. I'll be right over here if a question comes up." That's it. You acknowledge it, you remove the pressure, and you make it easy for them to come back to you when they're ready. And they will, far more often than you'd think, because you just did the one thing they weren't expecting: you didn't push.

What you don't do is try to overcome it. The salesperson who hears "just looking" and immediately starts firing questions or steering them to a vehicle confirms every fear the customer walked in with. Now the shield goes all the way up. Patience is the play. Give them the space and keep the door open.

It's Information — So Read It

Here's the part that separates the pros. "I'm just looking" tells you something needs to adjust — but not always the same something. Sometimes it's your approach: you came on too strong and you need to back off. Sometimes it's timing: they genuinely just started and need to look before they can talk. And sometimes it has nothing to do with you at all.

FROM THE FLOOR

I had a colleague who couldn't get any traction with a woman on the used car lot. She kept saying she was just looking. He couldn't figure out what was off — he'd done everything right as far as he could tell. He came and got me.

I went out, introduced myself, and asked how I could help her.

She said: "God, thank you. I really want to buy this car. But that other guy looks exactly like my ex-husband, and I cannot stand the sight of him."

Nothing to do with the car. Nothing to do with the approach. She knew exactly what she wanted — she just needed a different person in front of her before she was going to let the conversation happen. We tested the vehicle, worked out fair numbers, and she drove home happy.

Don't take "I'm just looking" personally. Don't take it as a verdict. Take it as information — something needs to adjust. Sometimes that's your approach. Sometimes it's giving more space. And occasionally it's a different person entirely. All of those are workable. None of them are the end of the deal.

That's the one that taught me to never take it personally. My colleague did everything right and still got "just looking" — because the reason had nothing to do with him or his approach. It was a face that reminded her of somebody she couldn't stand. He couldn't have fixed that by selling harder. The only fix was a different person walking out there. He read it as rejection and gave up. It wasn't rejection. It was information, and the information was: this customer needs something to change before she opens up. Once it changed, she bought.

None of It Is the End

So when you hear "just looking," run through it. Is it my approach? Then soften. Is it timing? Then give space. Is it something I can't see and can't control? Then maybe it's not even mine to fix. All three are workable. None of them is the end of the deal. The only way "just looking" actually ends a deal is if you let it run you off. So don't.

"The Rule: 'I'm just looking' isn't a verdict. It's information. Don't take it personally — take it as a sign that something needs to adjust."

CHAPTER 8

ASKING QUESTIONS WITHOUT INTERROGATING

You've got to ask questions. That's how you find out what the customer needs. But there's a right way and a wrong way, and the wrong way feels to the customer exactly like an interrogation—and nobody opens up to an interrogation.

This was my worst habit when I started. I'd been taught to qualify the customer, so I qualified them like a cop. Budget? Trade-in? Are you financing? How's your credit? Buying today? Bang, bang, bang, one after another, before they'd even told me their name. I thought I was being thorough. I was being a checklist with legs, and customers shut down on me cold.

Curiosity vs. Interrogation

The difference between curiosity and an interrogation isn't the questions. It's the spirit behind them, and the customer can feel which one you've got.

An interrogation is a list. You've got information you need to collect, and you march through it no matter what the customer says, because you're serving your checklist, not the conversation. Curiosity is the opposite. You ask because you actually want to know, and your next question comes from their last answer, not from a form in your head.

A customer can tell instantly which one is happening. The checklist feels like it's being processed. Curiosity feels like being listened to. One closes them down. The other opens them up.

One Question at a Time

The simplest fix is to slow down and ask one question at a time. Ask it, then actually wait for the whole answer, then respond to what they said before you ask anything else. That rhythm — question, listen, respond, question — is what makes it feel like a conversation instead of an interview.

When a customer tells you something, do something with it before you move on. They say they need better gas mileage. Don't just file it and fire the next question. Say "yeah? lot of highway driving?" Now you're following them, not your list. And the follow-up gets you better information than the next checklist item ever would have.

Give Before You Take

Another thing that keeps it from feeling like an interrogation: don't make the customer the only one talking. Drop in something useful between questions. Make an observation, share a quick relevant fact, react to what they said. A conversation goes both ways. If every single thing out of your mouth is a question, of course, it feels like an interrogation — you've turned them into the suspect and yourself into the detective.

The Information Comes Anyway

Here's what new salespeople don't believe until they see it: you get more information by asking less. When you stop interrogating and start having a real conversation, customers volunteer the stuff you used to have to pry out of them. Budget, timeline, what's really driving the purchase — it comes out on its own, because they trust you enough to say it. The interrogation gets you guarded, half-true answers. The conversation gets you the truth. Slow down, follow their lead, and let it come.

"The Rule: Curiosity earns answers. An interrogation kills them. Ask one real question, listen, and let the next one come from what they said."

Chapter 9

Creating Momentum Without Pressure

There's a moment in the first five minutes where the conversation is going well, the customer's talking, trust is building — and you have to decide what to do with it. Most salespeople do one of two wrong things. They either sit there and let the good conversation stall, going nowhere, until the customer says, "Well, thanks," and leaves. Or they slam on the gas and start pushing, and they kill the very thing they just built.

There's a third option, and it's the whole game: momentum without pressure. Keep things moving forward without ever making the customer feel pushed.

Momentum Is Not Pressure

First, get clear on the difference, because salespeople constantly confuse these two. Pressure is about you — your need to close, your urgency, your quota. The customer feels it as a shove. Momentum is about them — it's the natural next step in helping them get what they came for. The customer feels it as progress.

Same direction, totally different feel. Pressure makes a customer dig in. Momentum makes them lean forward. The difference is whether the next move serves your agenda or theirs.

Forward Motion Comes From Their Answers

Here's how you create momentum, honestly: you build the next step from what the customer just told you. They said they need something safe for the new baby and good on gas. You don't pitch. You say, "Let me show you the one I'd put my own family in"—and you start walking. That's momentum. It's not pressure, because it came straight out of what they told you they wanted. You're just taking the obvious next step toward solving their problem.

When the next move flows from their own words, it doesn't feel like a sale. It feels like help. And help has all the forward motion you need.

Small Yeses

Momentum builds on small agreements. Not the big "are you buying today?" —small, easy, honest yeses along the way. "Sounds like space is the big thing, yeah?" Yes. "Want to see the one that fits that best?" Yes. Each little yes is the customer agreeing to take one more step with you, of their own free will. String enough of those together and you've got real momentum, and not once did you push.

The trick is that every yes has to be genuine. You're not tricking them into agreeing. You're confirming you understand and inviting the next step. If they say no, that's information too—back up and find out what you missed.

Don't Outrun the Trust

The one way to blow it is to move faster than the trust you've built. Momentum only works while the customer's still with you. The second you get ahead of them — push for a step they're not ready for — it stops being momentum and becomes pressure, and you're right back to losing them.

So keep reading them, the way we talked about. Match their pace. Take the next step when they're ready, not when your commission wants it. Done right, the customer never feels pushed for a second. They just feel like they're making good progress with somebody who gets it. That's exactly what you want them to feel.

"The Rule: Momentum isn't pressure. It's the natural next step, offered at the right moment, by somebody the customer already trusts."

CHAPTER 10

MOVING FROM CONVERSATION TO THE VEHICLE

AT SOME POINT, THE talking has to turn into a car. You can have the best conversation on the lot, but if you never move it to an actual vehicle, you've just had a nice chat, and the customer goes home. The first five minutes are supposed to point somewhere, and where they point is a specific car the customer can see, touch, and sit in.

The question is when, and how, to make that move — without it feeling like the bait-and-switch the customer's been braced for the whole time.

The Move Comes When the Vehicle Answers Them

You make the move when you've heard enough to know what actually fits. Not before. The whole point of the conversation was to find out what they need—the real reason, the real problem. Once you've got that, the vehicle isn't a pivot away from the conversation. It's the answer to it.

That's the mindset shift. You're not changing the subject from "their needs" to "this car." You're showing them the car that answers their needs. "You said you haul a trailer on weekends, and the kids need room during the week — come look at this, it does both." The vehicle continues the conversation. It doesn't interrupt it.

Stop Talking and Start Walking

When you know what fits, stop talking about it and stand next to it. There's a point where more conversation is just stalling, and the strongest move is physical: "Let me show you"—and you walk. Get them moving toward the actual vehicle with you. Standing in the showroom describing a truck is nothing. Standing next to the truck with your hand on the bed rail is everything.

Movement creates its own momentum. A customer walking with you toward a car is more engaged than a customer standing still listening to you talk about one. Get them on their feet and headed toward the metal.

Connect the Car to What They Told You

At the vehicle, don't recite the brochure. Connect the car back to the exact things they told you they needed. They mentioned the long commute — pointing to the fuel numbers and the comfortable seat. They mentioned the new baby—open the back door and show them how the car seat fits. Every feature you point out should tie back to something they said in the conversation. That's what makes it land. You're not selling features. You're showing them their own words, answered.

This is also the payoff for all that listening. If you listened carefully in the first few minutes, this part is easy—you already know exactly what to point at. If you didn't listen, you're standing at a random car guessing, and the customer can tell.

Let Them Touch It

Once you're there, get them involved with the vehicle. Open the doors. Get them in the seat. Let them put their hands on it. A customer sitting in the driver's seat with their hands on the wheel is in a completely different place than one standing on the lot with their arms crossed. The car stops being an idea and starts being theirs. That's the whole reason you moved the conversation here. Now you're close to the next step—actually getting them to drive it.

"The Rule: When you've found what they're after, stop talking about it and go stand next to it. The conversation moves to the vehicle the moment the vehicle answers what they told you."

CHAPTER 11

EARNING THE TEST DRIVE

T HE TEST DRIVE IS where the real selling starts. Everything up to here — the greeting, the conversation, finding the real reason, moving to the vehicle — it's all been getting the customer ready for this. Once a customer drives the car, everything changes. It stops being a car on a lot and starts being the car they were just driving. That's powerful, and it's why getting them behind the wheel is the goal of the first five minutes.

But you don't get the test drive by asking for it cold. You earn it. And when you've earned it, you don't really have to ask at all.

Why the Drive Changes Everything

There's a reason the test drive matters so much. Reading about a car, looking at a car, even sitting in a car — none of it compares to driving it. Behind the wheel, the customer stops evaluating and starts imagining. They picture their commute. They picture the kids in the back. They picture pulling into their own driveway. The car quietly becomes theirs in their head, and that's a shift you can't create any other way.

That's why a salesperson who gets people driving outsells one who keeps people standing on the lot. The drive does work that no amount of talking can do.

You Have to Earn It First

Here's where new salespeople rush. They want to get the customer in the car so badly that they offer the drive too early, before they've earned it, and it feels like exactly what it is—a tactic to escalate. The customer pulls back.

You earn the test drive with everything that came before. By the time you offer it, the customer should trust you, feel heard, and be standing at a vehicle that actually fits what they told you they needed. If all that's true, the drive is the obvious next step, and it feels natural. If it's not true — if you skipped the conversation, didn't find the real reason, grabbed a random car — then the offer feels premature, because it is.

So earn it. Do the first five minutes right, and the test drive isn't a leap. It's the next step.

Offer It Like It's Obvious

When you've earned it, don't ask for it like you're asking a favor. Offer it like it's the natural next thing — because by now it is. "Let's take it around the block so you can feel how it drives." Not "would you maybe want to take a test drive, possibly?" The first sounds like somebody who knows this is the obvious step. The second sounds like somebody hoping for permission, and that hesitation makes the customer hesitate too.

Confidence here isn't pushy. It's just you treating the drive as the normal next part of the process, which is what it is. Hand them the keys like it's the most natural thing in the world.

Hand Off to the Real Process

And that's the threshold. The test drive marks the end of the first five minutes and the start of the real sales process. Your job in those opening minutes was never to close — it was to build enough trust, find enough truth, and create enough momentum that the customer gets in the car willingly. Get them driving, and you've done your job. Everything after that — the numbers, the trade, the close — is the rest of the process, and it's a whole lot easier when the first five minutes set it up right.

That's the entire point of this book. The first five minutes don't sell the car. They earn the test drive that does.

"The Rule: You don't ask for the test drive. You earn it — and once you have, you offer it like it's the obvious next thing, because by then it is."

Chapter 12

Where the First Five Minutes Go Wrong

We've spent this whole book on what to do. Now let's talk about what goes wrong, because knowing the mistakes is how you stop making them. And here's the thing about the first five minutes — they rarely get blown by one giant blunder. They get blown by small things, done over and over, that quietly run customers off. I made every one of these. Let me save you the years it took me to figure them out.

Never Making the Hand-Off

The most common failure is the one we started with: nailing the greeting and then freezing. The salesperson says hello and just stops—no hand-off, no opening question, no on-ramp. The customer's left standing in silence, so they do what people do with an awkward silence on a car lot — they escape into "just looking" and drift away. A good greeting with no hand-off is a dead end.

Talking Too Much

Right behind it is talking too much. Nervous salespeople fill every silence, pitch features nobody asked about, and never give the customer room to say a word. We covered this — the first five minutes belong to the customer. Every minute you spend talking is a minute you're not learning what you actually need to know. If you walk away from the first five minutes having done most of the talking, you did it wrong.

Interrogating

The flip side is interrogating — firing qualifying questions like a checklist before you've earned a single answer. Budget, trade, credit, buying today. It makes the customer feel processed instead of helped, and the guard goes up. Curiosity opens people. Interrogation closes them. If your questions are coming off a form in your head instead of out of what they just said, you're interrogating.

Pushing Past the Trust

Then there's pushing — moving faster than the trust you've built. The customer's warming up, things are going fine, and the salesperson gets greedy and lunges for the next step too soon. The second a customer feels pushed, momentum turns into pressure, and they pull back. You have to earn each step. Outrun the trust, and you lose the customer.

Prejudging the Customer

Here's one that cost me real money early on. I'd size a customer up in the first ten seconds — the way they were dressed, the car they drove in, whatever — and decide whether they were worth my time. I was wrong constantly. The guy in work clothes pays cash. The taxi customer buys in forty-five minutes. You never know who's a buyer, so you treat every single one like they are. Prejudging isn't just rude. It's bad business.

Ignoring the Quiet One

When there's more than one person, the mistake is selling to the talker and ignoring the quiet one. The quiet one's often the one who decides, and if they feel invisible, they'll kill the deal later, where you can't see it. Include everybody. The person not talking is still voting.

Taking "Just Looking" as a Verdict

And the big one we already covered: hearing "I'm just looking" and treating it as a final no. It's not a verdict, it's information. The salesperson who gives up on it walks away from deals that were sitting right there. The one who reads it and adjusts keeps the door open.

The Fix Is in the Small Things

Notice none of these are dramatic. There's no single catastrophic mistake that loses the deal. It's small things — a few too many words, one too-soon push, a quiet person left out, a brush-off taken personally. The good news is that small problems have small fixes. Talk a little less. Wait a little longer. Include the quiet one. Don't take the shield personally. Tighten up the small things, and you'll be amazed how many deals stop slipping through your fingers.

"The Rule: Most first five minutes don't go wrong with a big mistake. They go wrong with small ones — talking too much, pushing too soon, listening too little. Fix the small things and the deals stop slipping away."

Chapter 13

Putting It All Together: The First Five Minutes Done Right

We've taken the first five minutes apart, piece by piece. Now let's put it back together and watch it run as one clean motion, because in real life, it doesn't happen in separate steps. It happens in one smooth flow — and when it's done right, it barely looks like selling at all.

Let me walk you through it the way it actually goes.

The Whole Thing, Start to Finish

The customer arrives. You greet them right — no pouncing, no sprinting across the lot. Then you hand it off: a warm, easy opening that invites them to talk. "Glad you came in — what's got you out today?" And then you shut up and let them answer.

They start talking, and you listen — really listen — and your follow-ups come from what they say, not from a script. You're not interrogating. You're curious. As they open up, you're hunting for the real reason they came, the thing under the surface, and when you find it, you acknowledge it before you do anything else. All the while you're reading their pace and matching it, and you're being a real person, which is building the kind of trust that gets you honest answers.

Once you understand what they actually need, you make the move to the vehicle — not as a pivot, but as the answer to what they told you. You walk them to it. You tie it back to their own words. You get them touching it, sitting in it. And because you've earned it, the test drive is the obvious next step, so you offer it like the natural thing it is. They get in the car. The first five minutes are over, and the real sales process is underway.

That's the whole model. Greeting, hand-off, opening question, listening, the real reason, trust, pace, momentum, the vehicle, the drive. In practice, it's not ten steps. It's one conversation that flows.

FROM THE FLOOR

One afternoon, a customer pulled into the lot in a taxi. That caught my attention — most people drive themselves in. This one stepped out and walked directly toward a specific vehicle like he already knew exactly what he was looking for.

I didn't rush. I stood up, walked out at a normal pace, gave him a small wave as I crossed the lot. When I reached him, I introduced myself and told him I'd be glad to help if he had any questions.

He told me he'd just gotten off a flight and came straight from the airport. His vehicle had been destroyed in a fire in the parking lot while he was traveling. He'd seen one of our ads and came directly to us. He knew which vehicle he wanted. He just needed to drive it and confirm it.

We took a short test drive. Came back. He asked how to make out the check.

Start to finish, maybe forty-five minutes. The deal was easy because the approach was right. No pressure, no assumptions, no rushing. Just a professional greeting and a willingness to follow the customer's lead.

Not every customer comes in that ready to buy. But every customer deserves that same professional opening. You never know which one is going to be the taxi customer — the one who's already decided and just needs someone to not get in their way.

Look at how clean that is. He pulled in, I didn't rush, I greeted him at a normal pace, I introduced myself, and I let him lead. He told me the real reason — his vehicle burned up while he was traveling and he needed a replacement now. I didn't interrogate him. I didn't pitch him. I followed his lead, we drove it, and he asked how to make out the check. Forty-five minutes. The deal was easy because the approach was right. No pressure, no assumptions, no rushing.

It Won't Always Be That Easy — and That's Fine

Now, most customers don't show up already decided like the taxi customer did. Most need more conversation, more trust, more time to surface the real reason. That's fine. The point of that story isn't that every deal takes forty-five minutes. It's that every customer deserves the same professional opening — the same calm, unhurried, listen-first approach — whether they're ready to buy in forty-five minutes or forty-five days.

You never know which one is the taxi customer. So you treat everyone like they might be: greet them right, hand it off, listen, find the real reason, build the trust, and move toward the drive. Do that every time, and the ready ones close fast and the unready ones come back. Either way, you win more than you lose.

This Is the End of the Series

This is the last chapter of the last book, so let me tie the whole thing off. Across this series, we started at the very beginning — finding the nerve to approach a customer, making a clean first impression, getting the greeting right. This book took the next step: turning that greeting into a real conversation that points at a sale. That's the bridge, and now you know how to cross it.

You've got the whole arc now. Walk up to the customer the right way. Turn the hello into a conversation. Listen your way to the real reason they came. Build trust, match their pace, create momentum, and earn the drive. None of it is a trick. All of it is just being a professional who helps a person get what they came for. Do that, and you won't just survive in car sales. You'll be good at it. That's what this whole series was for.

"The Rule: Done right, the first five minutes don't feel like selling at all. They feel like a professional helping a person get what they came for — and that's exactly what closes the deal."

CONCLUSION

Here's the whole book in one breath: the greeting gets you in the door, and the next five minutes decide whether there's a deal behind it.

I spent a long time believing the sale was won at the close. It isn't. It's won — or lost — in those first few minutes after hello, when a customer is deciding whether you're somebody worth talking to. Get those minutes right, and the rest of the process gets easier. Get them wrong, and there's nothing to close.

Everything in this book comes down to a handful of simple things, and none of them are tricks. Hand off the greeting into a real conversation. Ask the kind of question that opens a door. Then listen — really listen — because the first five minutes belong to the customer, not to you. Find the real reason they came, which is almost never the reason they say first. Build trust by being a person instead of a routine. Read them and match their pace. Keep things moving without ever pushing. And when you've earned it, walk them to the vehicle and into the drive.

That's it. That's the first five minutes done right.

This is the last book in the series, so I'll leave you with the thing I most want you to take from all of it. The salespeople who last in this business aren't the slickest talkers or the hardest closers. They're the ones who treat customers like people and actually help them get what they came for. That's not soft. It's the most effective thing you can do, and it happens to be the right thing too. Do that, every customer, every time, and you'll be just fine.

Now go turn your next greeting into a conversation.

Tips for the Sales Manager

A note to the managers reading this, because the first five minutes aren't only a salesperson problem. They're a floor-culture problem, and that's on you.

Your people will do the first five minutes the way you train them and the way you model them. If your culture rewards fast pitches and hard pushes, that's what you'll get, and you'll wonder why customers keep walking. If you build a culture around handing off the greeting, listening first, and treating every customer like a buyer, that's what you'll get instead — and your numbers will show it.

Train the Hand-Off Directly

Most salespeople have never practiced the five seconds after hello. Role-play it. Make them get reps on turning a greeting into a conversation, because nobody's born knowing how.

Watch for the Interrogators

Your newer people will default to firing qualifying questions like a checklist. Catch it early and retrain it before it becomes a habit that costs them deals for years.

Kill the Prejudging

If your floor sizes up customers by what they're wearing or what they drove in on, you're leaking money. Remember the taxi customer. Make it a rule: every customer gets the same professional opening, period.

Protect the Quiet Ones

Teach your people to include everybody in the conversation, especially the person who isn't talking — because that's frequently the one who decides.

Model It Yourself

The story about the furniture store wasn't a sales problem; it was a culture problem, and it started at the top. Your people are watching how you treat customers. Treat everyone like they matter, and they'll do the same. The first five minutes are learnable. Your job is to make sure they get learned.

APPENDIX

The Rules

Every Rule from this book, collected in one place. Read them straight through whenever you need a quick reset before you hit the floor.

Introduction

The greeting gets you in the door. The next five minutes decide whether there's a deal behind it.

Chapter 1 — The Hand-Off

A greeting isn't a conversation. The hand-off is the move that turns one into the other.

Chapter 2 — The Opening Question

Ask the question that opens a door, not the one that slams it. "What's got you out today" beats "What are you here to buy" every time.

Chapter 3 — Listen First

The first five minutes belong to the customer. The salesperson who listens first outsells the one who talks first.

Chapter 4 — Finding the Real Reason They Came

Nobody buys a car. They buy what the car fixes. Find the real reason they came, and you've found the deal.

Chapter 5 — Building Real Trust, Not Small Talk

Trust isn't built with small talk. It's built by being a real person and proving you actually heard them.

Chapter 6 — Reading the Customer and Matching Their Pace

Match the customer's pace, not your script. The fast ones want answers; the slow ones want room. Give them theirs, not yours.

Chapter 7 — "I'm Just Looking"

"I'm just looking" isn't a verdict. It's information. Don't take it personally — take it as a sign that something needs to adjust.

Chapter 8 — Asking Questions Without Interrogating

Curiosity earns answers. An interrogation kills them. Ask one real question, listen, and let the next one come from what they said.

Chapter 9 — Creating Momentum Without Pressure

Momentum isn't pressure. It's the natural next step, offered at the right moment, by somebody the customer already trusts.

Chapter 10 — Moving from Conversation to the Vehicle

When you've found what they're after, stop talking about it and go stand next to it. The conversation moves to the vehicle the moment the vehicle answers what they told you.

Chapter 11 — Earning the Test Drive

You don't ask for the test drive. You earn it — and once you have, you offer it like it's the obvious next thing, because by then it is.

Chapter 12 — Where the First Five Minutes Go Wrong

Most first five minutes don't go wrong with a big mistake. They go wrong with small ones — talking too much, pushing too soon, listening too little. Fix the small things, and the deals stop slipping away.

Chapter 13 — Putting It All Together

Done right, the first five minutes don't feel like selling at all. They feel like a professional helping a person get what they came for — and that's exactly what closes the deal.

Also Available

Flagship

The Complete Car Sales Survival Guide — The No-BS Playbook for New Automotive Salespeople

The Car Sales Survival Guide Series

Book 1 — The Meet and Greet Playbook — How to Make Powerful First Impressions with Customers, Clients, and Guests

Book 2 — The First 60 Seconds in Car Sales — A Proven Meet and Greet System to Build Trust and Start More Conversations

Book 3 — How to Handle "I'm Just Looking" in Car Sales — A Simple System to Turn Brush-Offs into Productive Conversations

Book 4 — Body Language in Car Sales — How Posture, Eye Contact, and Presence Build Customer Trust

Book 5 — Greeting Customers on the Lot — How to Approach Buyers Without Pressure

Book 6 — The Ten-Second Rule in Car Sales — Why First Impressions Determine Whether Customers Stay or Leave

Book 7 — The Car Sales Conversation Starter Guide — How to Begin Natural Conversations That Lead to Sales

Book 8 — Car Sales Confidence for New Salespeople — How to Approach Customers Without Fear or Hesitation

Book 9 — Common Car Sales Greeting Mistakes — What Drives Customers Away in the First Minute

Book 10 — The First Five Minutes With a Car Buyer — How to Transition from Greeting to Conversation and Move Toward the Sale

WORK WITH BRUCE

If you're interested in one-on-one coaching, sales team training, or dealership consulting, Bruce works with individuals and organizations through Life Guidance Consulting.

For inquiries:

www.lifeguidanceconsulting.com

bruce@lifeguidanceconsulting.com

For publishing inquiries or bulk orders:

www.bedrockheritagepublishing.com

info@bedrockheritagepublishing.com

About the Author

Bruce Huddleston spent thirty-five years in the automotive industry, working every level of the business from showroom floor salesperson to finance manager, sales manager, used car manager, and general manager. His career included new-car franchise dealerships, independent used-car operations, and a decade in buy-here, pay-here — giving him a breadth of experience that few in the industry can match.

He began as a high school dropout who needed a job and ended up discovering a profession. He ended as a veteran who had trained hundreds of salespeople, managed multiple departments, and built a reputation for straight talk in an industry that doesn't always reward it.

Since retiring, Bruce has opened a life coaching practice, assists his wife with her mental health therapy practice, and operates Bedrock Heritage Publishing, a division of Life Guidance Consulting LLC, where he writes practical guides for sales professionals across multiple industries.

The Complete Car Sales Survival Guide is his flagship work. The Car Sales Survival Guide Series — a collection of focused training guides on specific sales skills — is built on the same foundation of real experience, honest insight, and zero tolerance for the kind of nonsense that gives sales a bad name.

He lives in Tyler, Texas.

A Quick Favor

If The First Five Minutes With a Car Buyer helped you — if it changed how you walk onto a lot, how you read a customer, or how you think about what your body is saying before you open your mouth — I'd be grateful if you'd take two minutes to leave a review wherever you bought it.

Reviews matter more than most people realize. They help other salespeople find books that can actually make a difference in their work. And honest feedback helps me keep writing things worth reading.

You can simply scan the QR code below.

https://www.amazon.com/review/create-review/?asin=1972179187

www.bedrockheritagepublishing.com

Thank you for spending time with this book. Now go to work.

— Bruce Huddleston

9 781972 179185